Sinead Collins.

CM01602894

When People Die

by Teresa Dcaccia
with illustrations by Kati Teague

Matthew James Publishing Ltd

When People Die

by Teresa Dcaccia
with illustrations by Kati Teague

First published in 2003 on behalf of
Rainbows-Great Britain & Rainbows-Ireland
by
Matthew James Publishing Ltd
19 Wellington Close, Chelmsford, Essex CM1 2EE
www.matthew-james.co.uk

ISBN 1898366 82 9

Design by Eclipse
Printed by Gallpen Colour Print, Norwich

RAINBOWS is a non-profit making, international organisation that provides training for establishing peer support groups for children, adolescents, and adults who have experienced a death, divorce, or any other painful transition in their family.
For further information see pp 38-39 or contact:

RAINBOWS-GREAT BRITAIN
17 Market Square
Higham Ferrers
Northants. NN10 8DJ
01933 355175
rainbows.dc@virgin.net

RAINBOWS-IRELAND
Loreto Centre
Crumlin Road
Dublin.
01-4734175
rainbows@eircom.net

To
my Grandfather, Herbert Chambers,
for his bravery and his fears and all that
made him special.

John and Laura were brother and sister. John was six years old and Laura was five years old.

John and Laura did everything together. They were never apart. They went to school together, and they came home together. They would even play in the playground together.

In the winter they would wrap up warmly in their coats, hats and gloves. Then they would go outside and slip and slide on the frosty ground.

In the spring, they would feed the ducks in the park together.

In the summer they would sit on the grass and have a picnic.

25

In the autumn they would jump up and down in the leaves, and throw them at each other.

John and Laura were the best of friends. They loved being together. But then one day their mum told John that Laura was very sick, and that she needed lots of rest.

Laura didn't go to school anymore. She stayed in bed all the time. John felt very lonely, but he looked forward to the day when Laura would be well again.

LAURA'S
ROOM

But Laura never did get better. One day John's mum and dad told him that Laura had died.

John couldn't believe it. Laura could not be dead.

But she was!

John was very sad for a long time. He felt so alone. John missed Laura every day. He thought that he would never be happy again.

LAURA'S
ROOM

Winter, spring, summer and autumn went by and John was still sad.
He would sit in the playground all alone until one day a boy in John's class sat beside him. John quite enjoyed talking to him. They quickly became good friends

Time went by very slowly, but John's new friend made him feel a little better. They would play together and sometimes they would ride their bikes after school.
Slowly John learnt to smile again.

John began to see that although Laura had died, everything else had stayed the same.
Winter went by. So did spring, summer and autumn. Although Laura was not there to share them with John, they came and went in just the same way as they had before.

John would always miss Laura, but he would always have his good memories of her. Life went on and John got more and more used to not being with Laura.

Death is a part of life. Although it is sad when people die, we can still keep our memories of them.
Living and dying are both parts of the same thing, life.

Notes for Adults

Introduction

Children are a most precious gift. They carry a message of hope and continuation of life. A child's first teachers are parents who teach not only words and physical movement but also how to relate, how to care for others and how to love self. As the child develops physically and emotionally, she/he also develops feelings of security within the family. It is in the family situation where a child's personal identity is formed.

Children grow up assuming that the parents will always be there for them, providing them with protection, keeping them healthy and emotionally secure. When the death of a parent occurs or one parent moves out of the family home, or the divorce of parents takes place, the entire world of the child crashes down. They do not know what will happen next or who will care for them or if they will be abandoned by the remaining parent. They cannot imagine what their lives will be like in the future.

There are five books in this series, each dealing with a different aspect of the grief caused through various situations of loss.

The titles of the five books are:

Our Feelings -

Feelings can affect our lives and they can often be confusing. What we do with our feelings and how we express them is important to our future well-being.

It's Working -

Grief is a natural human feeling to any important loss situation. Only when it is faced can it be resolved.

When People Die -

Death is a part of life but this does not make bereavement any easier to bear.

Our Families -

Accepting that families come in all shapes and sizes is the first step to healthy relationships.

Getting Used to Change -

Adjusting to a new family can be an anxious time and can take a long time.

The definition of grief is deep sorrow. This can be caused by many situations of loss. The common causes of such grief among children are:

the death of a parent, grandparent or other family member,

the death of a sibling or friend,

the loss of a parent through parental separation, desertion or divorce,

the adjusting to a new family situation when the pain of loss is still raw, and

coping in an enforced lone parent family situation.

Teresa Dcaccia has written these stories sympathetically and set them in a child's world, using language and concepts that a child can easily understand. Whilst facing up to the major issues of divorce and death, she has also explored the issues of loss through other experiences such as moving house or a marriage in the family. The books can be adapted to any significant loss since the feelings experienced are often the same.

Kati Teague's illustrations provide a wonderful accompaniment to the stories, showing the full range of emotions experienced by children who are suffering loss.

By the use of these books, children may come to realise that they are not alone in their pain, that the feelings of grief now experienced will not last forever and that there is a rainbow after the storm.

Our Feelings

Children need to know that everyone has feelings. There are no right or wrong feelings. Feelings are a natural part of our lives. It is the responsibility of the individual person how feelings are expressed. Children who are able to express their feelings positively such as talking about them, find it easier to accept the situations they find themselves in.

The story of Amy shows how feelings of loss can affect one's well-being. The loss can be anything that produces the complex feelings of sadness and grief. Amy and her mother move house and this produces in Amy, feelings of loneliness, sadness, fear, anger and guilt.

The story moves forward to show how Amy begins to feel more content as she learns to talk about her feelings. Finally she is able to make new friends.

The key to moving forward is a recognition and sharing of the different emotions experienced. Such a scenario can be applied to any situation of grief and loss.

It's Working

Grief is the natural reaction to loss. The loss could be anything from moving house, or going to a new school to family separation, divorce or someone dying. As life progresses there are many such moments of grief that need to be faced. At such moments many people, especially children are frightened of their feelings. They do not know who to turn to for help. Many of them just try to bury the grief they feel.

Marie, the youngest member of a large family, experiences vague feelings of sadness on the wedding day of her elder brother, Tony. It dawns on her that her feelings of sadness are because she feels she has "lost" her brother who was like a leader among the diverse members of the family. Without him, family life seemed to suffer. Marie was very sad throughout this difficult time of change.

Gradually, however, other members began to assume the role that had once belonged to Tony and the family begin to get along better.

Changes in the family can be painful but things can get better.

When People Die

When someone dies, those left behind experience overwhelming feelings of loss. So begins a journey of grief through anguish, in loneliness and fear, tinged with all sorts of other emotions such as guilt and anger. There is no time scale. The journey may be long and hard but if worked through adequately, there will come a time when the sharp pain felt in the days and months immediately after the bereavement will give way to an acceptance of what has happened. This acceptance does not wipe away the pain but allows a moving forward, no longer overwhelmed by feelings of grief.

In the story of a brother and sister, the subject of death is handled with great sensitivity. John and Laura were inseparable. They went everywhere together. Then Laura fell ill and died. John was consumed with sadness and the sadness lasted a long time. John endured a long period of loneliness until he made a new friend at school.

Gradually, over a long time, he began to feel better. While he would never forget his sister, he came to realise that life moved on. The death of someone close is one of the most difficult moments in life but it is not the end. The hurt need not last forever.

Our Families

Children who experience loss in their family life need support as they try to come to terms with change. According to national statistics, in this first decade of the twenty-first century, 25% of children have seen their parents divorce and at least one in ten children are living in stepfamilies. Many children feel lonely and confused by this experience.

There are a growing number of new types of family situations in our society, so much so that some statisticians predict that the traditional marriage will be the minority form of family in the not too distant future.

When Mark goes to school he meets lots of new friends but also is made aware that there are lots of different types of families and that not everyone lives with Mum and Dad, brother and sister as he did.

The death of his grandmother brings the issue of the family to the surface and Mark begins to understand that all families are different, but that does not mean that one is more functional than any other.

Getting used to Change

The number of stepfamilies is on the increase and adjusting to the changes involved is not easy for children. They have to learn to cope with different rules and expectations, new surroundings, moving house and school, the isolation of leaving friends behind and getting used to stepbrothers and sisters, an experience that can be traumatic in itself.

Shane's parents are divorced and he is faced with the prospect of a stepmother, stepbrother and stepsister. Shane is confused by these changes in the family and finds life difficult and goes through a series of different feelings.

Gradually, after talking about his feelings, and communicating with his stepfamily, he begins to get used to the changes and moves towards accepting his new family.

RAINBOWS

What is RAINBOWS?

RAINBOWS is a non-profit making international organisation, offering training and programmes for establishing peer support groups in communities, schools, churches, and social agencies. The mission of RAINBOWS is to provide training and programmes for establishing peer support groups for children and adolescents who are grieving a death, separation, desertion, divorce or any other painful loss.

What programmes are available for children and young people?

RAINBOWS offers 2 programmes:

Rainbows (Primary Edition),

Spectrum (Adolescent Edition),

The Method

The RAINBOWS materials are designed to provide support as well as healing. Through them a great number of children and adolescents are assisted with personal encouragement and support which is unavailable in many other settings.

RAINBOWS helps by:

- encouraging children to rebuild their self esteem,
- enabling them to name, understand and come to terms with the many emotions they experience,
- reassuring those who have anxieties or feelings of guilt,
- encouraging young people to move towards forgiving those whom they feel have caused their pain,
- providing a group setting where children can share freely with each other,
- dealing with normal feelings associated with a stressful life event - grievous loss,
- providing a trained Facilitator who listens. The experience is dependent on deepening relationships within the group,
- offering acceptance, understanding and an exploration of a person's own coping skills,
- providing a safe setting in which children and adolescents can, with the help of a trained Facilitator, come to terms with the feelings they are experiencing,
- creating small groups in which all are experiencing similar feelings, and can work through the programmes, exploring and expressing their feelings of grief.

How a School can set up a RAINBOWS Group

- The school has to decide to become a SITE.
- Contact your RAINBOWS National Office

Rainbows - Great Britain National Office
17 Market Square,
Higham Ferrers,
Northants. NN10 8DJ
Tel: 01933 355175 Fax: 01933 355181
email: rainbows.dc@virgin.net
www.rainbowsgb.org

RAINBOWS-Ireland National Office
Loreto Centre
Crumlin Road
Dublin.
01-4734175
rainbows@eircom.net

Please consider becoming a RAINBOWS SITE to help Children pass:

. . . from hurt,
through healing,
to hope. . .